ARCHITECTURE
For the Birds

Joan Vorderbruggen   Darryl Booker   Cindy Urness

Theran Press

Theran Press is the academic publishing imprint of Silver Goat Media.

Theran is dedicated to authentic partnerships with our academic associates, to the quality design of a scholarly books, and to elite standards of peer review.

Theran seeks to free intellectuals from the confines of traditional publishing.

Theran scholars are authorities and revolutionaries in their respective fields.

Theran encourages new models for generating and distributing knowledge.

For our creatives. For our communities. For our world.

WWW.THERANPRESS.ORG

ARCHITECTURE FOR THE BIRDS. Copyright © 2016 by Joan Vorderbruggen, Darryl Brooker, and Cindy Urness, All rights reserved.

Published by Silver Goat Media, LLC, Fargo, ND 58108. This publication is protected by copyright, and permission should be obtained from the publisher prior to any reproduction, storage in a retrieval system, or transmission in any form or by any means, electronic, mechanical, photocopying, recording, or likewise. SGM books are available at discounts, regardless of quantity, for K-12 schools, non-profits, or other educational institutions. To obtain permission(s) to use material from this work, or to order in bulk, please submit a written request to Silver Goat Media, LLC, PO Box 2336 Fargo, ND 58108, or contact SGM directly at: info@silvergoatmedia.com.

This book was designed and produced by Silver Goat Media, LLC. Fargo, ND U.S.A.
www.silvergoatmedia.com
SGM, the SGM goat, Theran Press, and the Theran theta are trademarks of Silver Goat Media.

Cover and Interior Photographs - Darryl Booker and Nicholas Strombeck
Cover Design - Travis Klath and Nicholas Strombeck © 2016
This book was typeset in Helvetica by Travis Klath

ISBN-10: 1944296034
ISBN-13: 978-1944296032 (Silver Goat Media)

A portion of the proceeds from the sale of this book are donated to the Longspur Prairie Fund.
www.longspurprairie.org

2.0 - 170811

Printed and bound in the United States of America

TABLE OF CONTENTS

4	Introduction
5	The Pritzker Prize
6	The Problem
7	The Bird House Designs
31	Student Contributors
	Pritzker Laureates
32	Competition Winners
34	Competition Jury
	Faculty Advisors

INTRODUCTION

The birdhouse project was conceived as a way to introduce three important lessons to the design students in the architecture program at North Dakota State University:

1) When designing, look to the masters to understand how to develop a vision and commitment to design.
2) Understand the nature of your user and the place they reside.
3) Ideas are only useful when they are built well.

This book is a collection of birdhouse projects inspired by the most celebrated architects of the 20th and 21st century, and a select number of bird species who reside in and around the communities of Fargo, North Dakota, and Moorhead, Minnesota. These are the two muses students have been asked to study and interpet as they create their own version of the classic, backyard "birdhouse" for these species who willingly occupy "man-made" structures.

The project is treated as a design competition, where students have two weeks to design and build the birdhouses. The projects are put on exhibit at the Plains Art Museum, Fargo, North Dakota for a period of several weeks where the public has an opportunity to see the work.

In addition, an outside jury of experts is assembled, the projects are reviewed, and winners are selected.

THE PRITZKER PRIZE

The international prize, which is awarded each year to an architect/s for significant achievement, was established by the Pritzker family of Chicago through their Hyatt Foundation in 1979. It is granted annually and is often referred to as "architecture's Nobel" and "the profession's highest honor."

THE PROBLEM

Architects have a long history of designing objects other than buildings. Whether it is the design of furniture, eating utensils, or textiles, it is important that the architect understands WHO s/he is designing for, and WHAT needs to be considered in the design. It is no different when designing for any living creature.

The challenge is to come up with a creative design solution for a birdhouse, realized through the actual construction of a dwelling suitable for a chosen bird or "client." This is a small-scale design-build project – an opportunity to actually construct a dwelling, with a focus on design, originality, and project craft, and to be inhabited by a living thing!

Beginning with the initial exploration of a selected award-winning architect, "channel" his or her design philosophy into a design methodology, translate the philosophy into an original space and form, and construct this design into a house for a specific regional bird. Knowledge of bird requirements and regional habitat are critical to the habitability of the houses created. The birdhouses are judged according to: 1) interpretation of design philosophy of Pritzker architect, 2) knowledge and understanding of bird specie designing for, and 3) material and craft of the house.

Bird/Client: Tree Swallow
Pritzker Architect: James Stirling

AARON CODDEN

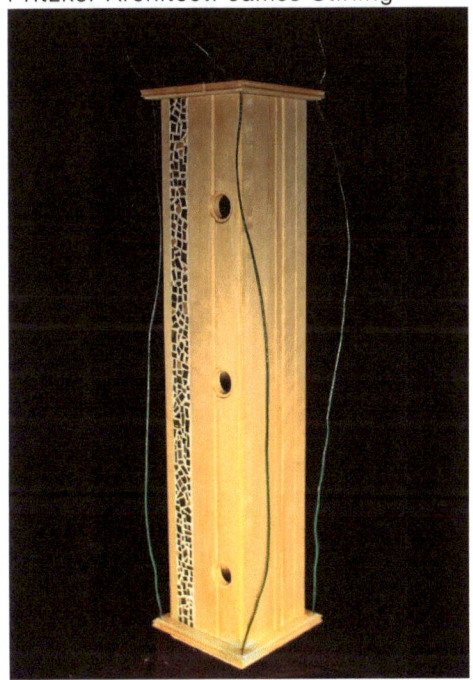

The inspiration for this birdhouse was the verticality of the Engineering Center at the University of Leicester designed by James Stirling. This architect focuses on community spaces that interlock and stack in order to create a tight-knit community. I designed my birdhouse with three holes, allowing for the tree swallows to nest in flocks and maintain a sense of comradery and community.

Bird/Client: Northern Flicker
Pritzker Architect: Shigeru Ban

ALEX MALNAA

The birdhouse was inspired in part by Shigeru Ban's work with woven materials and the tulip. The origin of the word tulip stems from the word for woven gauze in Turkish, tülbend. Attached at only two points, the "petals" are able to move freely within their woven pattern, blooming to reveal the log for the Northern Flicker to use as its home.

Bird/Client: Eastern Bluebird
Pritzker Architect: Oscar Niemeyer

ALEXANDRA MILLS

Oscar Niemeyer is a modernist celebrated for his love of sensual curves, elegant geometry and daring color. Following Niemeyer's fondness of rounded forms and staying true to his use of color, my birdhouse is made entirely of concrete, painted bright white with sensual red and yellow stripes, and cast in dimensions suitable for an Eastern Bluebird. My birdhouse design is intended to be a functional work of art for a happy Bluebird family.

Bird/Client: House Wren
Pritzker Architect: SANAA

BEN GILLIS

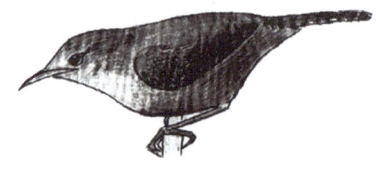

Kazuyo Sejima and Ryue Nishizawa design in such a way that a space isn't completed until the user makes it their own. I created a bird house that draws its form from the wren's unique motions, and catches the eye with its flowing form. But once a bird makes it home and fills it with its nest, it takes on a new feel. The nest subtly reflects the forest around it, merging the space the wren has created with the trees around it.

Bird/Client: Eastern Screech Owl
Pritzker Architect: Richard Rogers

BEN JOHNSON

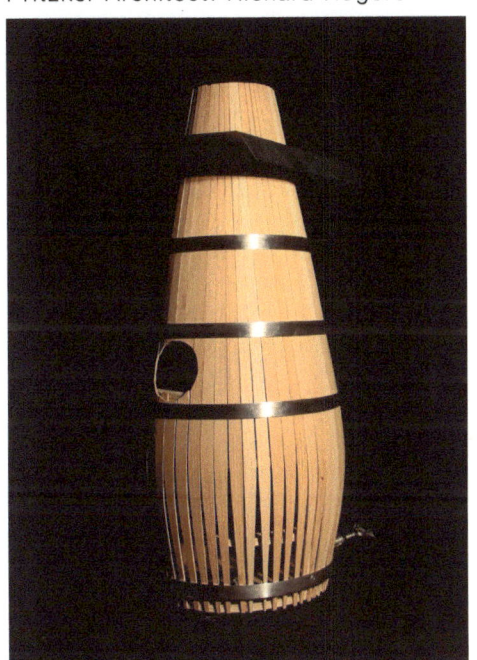

The barrel owl house is inspired by Richard Roger's Bordeaux Law Courts, a building where the individual court rooms are separate wood-clad pods with light entering at the top. In the barrel owl house, the individual barrel gives the owl its own space in the woods allowing him to get away from weather and other predators.

Bird/Client: House Wren
Pritzker Architect: Zaha Hadid

BRADY LAURIN

In designing a home for the House Wren, my inspiration came from the variety of organic forms that architect Zaha Hadid designs. Accented in the final design is a hive-like shape to relate the project back to nature. This "hive" also serves to represent the busy nature of the Wren, a very active bird.

Bird/Client: White Breasted Nuthatch
Pritzker Architect: Herzog + De Meuron

CHRIS WHITE

The inspiration for this project was to try and create an object that embodies both the simple geometric design of Herzog and De Meuron and the fast moving nature of the White Breasted Nuthatch. This birdhouse will blend into the natural surroundings, but still stand out and embody the ideas of nature. A key feature of this birdhouse is rather than having a standard small opening, it utilizes a larger, more cavern-like opening.

Bird/Client: Northern Flicker
Pritzker Architect: James Stirling

CHISTA GAILBREATH

James Stirling focused on two main principles when designing - the experience the interior spaces would provide and architecture as an art form. Stirling often emphasized the contrast between negative and positive space and a connection to history and the user's culture. This birdhouse relies on simplicity of form, natural materials, and strong negative spaces to create a customized habitat for Northern Flickers.

Bird/Client: Northern Flicker
Pritzker Architect: Fumihiko Maki

DANIEL TODD

My birdhouse was guided by the style of modernist Fumihiko Maki. The design features the symbolic shapes Maki uses in every project: the cross form (seen in blue glass tile) and stepped pyramid (surrounding the opening as a predator guard). I used a wood trim detail to articulate and organize these main elements. The vertical lines helped to establish asymmetrical balance, whereas the horizontal lines provided continuity from one side to the next.

Bird/Client: Eastern Bluebird
Pritzker Architect: Thom Mayne

DAVID WALBOLT

My architect was Thom Mayne and my bird was the Eastern Bluebird. Mayne is known for making his buildings and surrounding environments interpret each other, but with "attitude." The birdhouse is shaped to resemble the flow of grass in the prairie land as this is where bluebird typically live, and was built with old barn wood. I sharply angled two of the walls and contrasted the wood. I used the irregular shape of the wood to provide for a natural air flow for the birds.

Bird/Client: White Breasted Nuthatch
Pritzker Architect: Aldo Rossi

DREW WOLF

The inspiration for my birdhouse came from the design philosophies of Aldo Rossi. Rossi was known for his simple building forms that elicit memories of traditional architecture. My birdhouse incorporates a tree-trunk-like cylinder shape, with protruding spindles that represent branches. I was also inspired by the white-breasted nuthatch's ability to walk vertically up and down trees trunks, so I chose to flip the original shape, acknowledging that for the bird there is no up or down.

Bird/Client: Eastern Bluebird
Pritzker Architect: Richard Meier

ELIZABETH RAE

The inspiration for my birdhouse was Richard Meier and his Douglas House, where land-based ships, color, and light play an important role in the design. The inspiration for my design were the sails of a Chinese Sailing Vessel. Using the right triangle in repetition allowed me to create the fan like look, each piece set at a different angle and placed together in a playful nature. The paint choice was to make the house stand out from its surroundings, interesting to spot from afar.

Bird/Client: Northern Flicker
Pritzker Architect: Richard Meier

ELIZABETH THORDSTON

By combining the philosophy of Richard Meier and the needs of the Northern Flicker, I came up with the idea for the Richard Flicker House. This bird requires metal in their homes or in close proximity because it is used as a defense mechanism; the Northern Flicker uses its sharp beak to bang on metal with the intention of scaring away predators. The metal was painted white to reduce the sun glare reflected off the panels for the bird's safety but also because Richard Meier claims that white allows us to see all other colors more clearly and vibrantly.

Bird/Client: Black Capped Chickadee
Pritzker Architect: I.M. Pei

HAMZA ELAZHARI DAOUDI

Influenced by the geometric designs and simple historical references of I.M Pei, I designed Athens Birdhouse in way that merges inspirations and architectural influences. I also focused on gestalt psychology, by combining triangles, long design motifs on the façade, and rectangular openings on the side. The overall diamond shape of the birdhouse was inspired from the reflection of the Louvre Museum in Paris on the water around it.

Bird/Client: Eastern Bluebird
Pritzker Architect: Richard Meier

HANNAH LANGR

For me, inspiration came in a combination of the needs of the Eastern Bluebird and the design philosophy of Richard Meier. Primarily, the design is concerned with the safety and wellbeing of the bluebird as its conservation is crucial to the species. The construction methods involved creating walls out of smaller, modular pieces so as to emulate Meier's use of grids within large openings. He also inspired my use of white pickling stain to try and resolve the desire for light and the client's comfort.

Bird/Client: Eastern Screech Owl
Pritzker Architect: Glenn Murcutt

HUAXIN WEI

Based on Glenn Murcutt's architecture, I concluded that simple, linear, high frames are his major design elements. The Eastern Screech Owl loves cedar or raw pine wood. Similarly, Murcutt uses wood and other natural materials, especially that which is easily found around the site. Another Murcutt feature is the use of louvers so it became a signature exterior pattern for my design.

Bird/Client: American Kestrel
Pritzker Architect: Herzog + de Meuron

INGRID FULLERTON

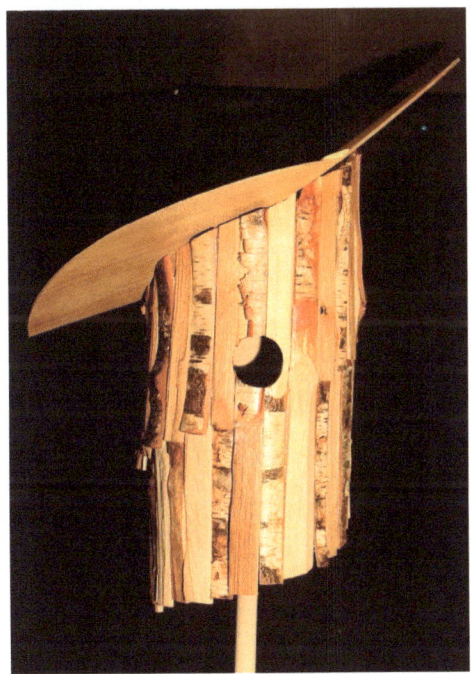

Herzog & de Meuron often apply representational geometry to select areas of a building and use innovative materials to unify it with its particular site, creating a site-responsive design. I was inspired by their Laban Centre for Music and Dance, in which they applied layers of colored glass to a curved building façade. For my birdhouse for the American Kestrel, I wanted to use materials which would seem appropriate to a wild setting, so I individually trimmed firewood logs to fit into a tongue-and-groove pattern, emphasizing the rough and knotty nature of the wood.

Bird/Client: Black Capped Chickadee
Pritzker Architect: Renzo Piano

JACOB HASSE

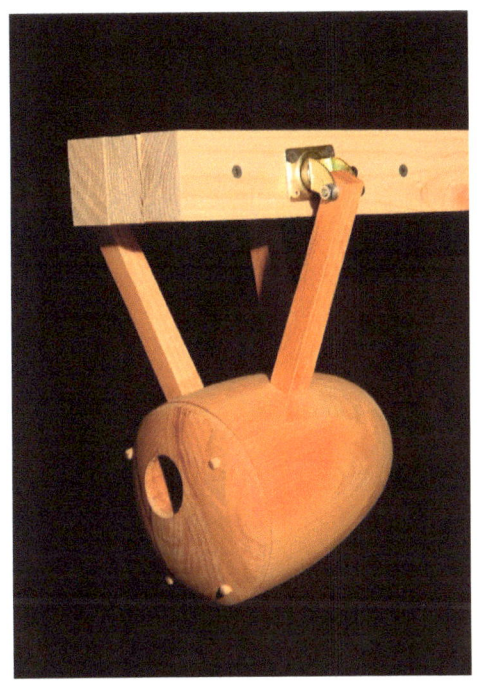

Mimicking the excavating nature of chickadees, the bird house is carved from a larger block of Alder and Cherry. Put to scale, the bird house portrays the vivacious nature of chickadees as the house tries to restrain the skyward growth of the tree. Drawing on inspiration from Renzo Piano's design philosophy and a case study of the Padre Pio Pilgrimage Church in San Giovanni Rotondo, Italy, this bird house serves as a home for the feathered and a form of timeless design.

Bird/Client: Tree Swallow
Pritzker Architect: Thom Mayne

JACOB PETERSON

My task was to design a birdhouse based on the work of Thom Mayne, which fits the needs of my bird and my client, the Tree Swallow. There is a layered quality to Mayne's work and many of his buildings seemed very simple on the most basic level, but are morphed and molded into something much more complex and unique. My design, Swallow Hollow, is a simple cube molded into something more useful.

Bird/Client: White Breasted Nuthatch
Pritzker Architect: Aldo Rossi

JAVAN ARROYO

Aldo Rossi's design philosophy focuses on the response of the architecture to the site, specifically how it fits into the context of its surrounding architecture. That is how I came up with the overall form of the birdhouse, with its location in the crook of a tree. The second point of inspiration was the White-breasted Nuthatch itself, and how the bird would respond to shapes and forms. I continued to ask myself how I could make something do more for the sake of the bird.

Bird/Client: Eastern Screech Owl
Pritzker Architect: Fumihiko Maki

JENNA HEGEDUS

I was inspired by Fumihiko Makis' ability to create large spaces while keeping them at a human scale, how he mixes traditional and modern Japanese Architecture, and how he create spaces, and then covers them from the exterior. I tried to apply these ideas within the interior space of the bird house, curving wood over the space. The two curved walls separate, representing the traditional aspects of Japanese culture, while at the same time creating a dynamic shape, representing the modernized ideas of architecture.

Bird/Client: Northern Flicker
Pritzker Architect: Rafael Moneo

JESSICA MEYER

The horizontality in Rafael Moneo's designs is subtle, so I decided to use layers of vertical "slabs" cut horizontally and then assembled back together to create the birdhouse. This allowed for the vertical element to be strong, while adding subtle horizontal lines that were indicative of Moneo. Beyond juxtaposition and compromise, I was mindful of the protection component necessary for the Northern Flicker.

Bird/Client: Eastern Screech Owl
Pritzker Architect: Peter Zumthor

JOHN KROLAK

I designed and built my Eastern Screech Owl house through the view of famous architect, Peter Zumthor. Inspired by Zumthor's design philosophy, I designed the nesting box with materials of the site and elements that would allow it to blend into the surrounding background.

Bird/Client: American Kestrel
Pritzker Architect: Richard Rogers

JON HEGSETH

The inspiration for my birdhouse came from Richard Rogers and his work on the Pompidou Centre. I was challenged by his strong use of exposed structure as a form of building façade and enclosure, creating a sense of honesty. I tried to incorporate this ideology into the building of my birdhouse – the Strongbox –through the use of the threaded rod, which holds the entire house together.

Bird/Client: American Kestrel
Pritzker Architect: Frank Gehry

JULIE RASANEN

The flight and fierce nature of the American Kestrel inspired the use of metal and the element of movement in making a dynamic form, similar to Frank Gehry's designs. The sloping metal roof represents the Kestrel taking off for flight, with an emphasis on form at the front of the house, similar to Gehry's work. The interior has scored walls to help the Kestrel climb, and has a tilted perch, which lets the bird search for prey.

Bird/Client: American Kestrel
Pritzker Architect: Norman Foster

KAITLYN ABERLE

Norman Foster's architectural language of basic geometric shapes, repetition, and exposed structure inspired the shape and function of the design. The use of minimal glass "windows" on the facade and the slit on the roof create a hint of natural light that gives life to the interior, and allows for ventilation and drainage, making a cozy place for the American Kestrel to nest.

Bird/Client: American Kestrel
Pritzker Architect: Tadao Ando

KELSEY JARRETT

The Church of the Light by Tadao Ando inspired my design, with its use of reinforced concrete, sensitive treatment of natural light, and engagement with nature. The light within the structure changes as the sun moves throughout the day, creating a contrast between dark and light. Ando's precision and craft in his use of concrete influenced the roof, where American Kestrels tend to sit and interact.

Bird/Client: Black Capped Chickadee
Pritzker Architect: Norman Foster

KENNETH STEPHENSON

The reoccurring themes of Norman Foster's work were both sustainability and structure, inspiring me to use geometries, shapes, and angles to make a boxy birdhouse into an artistic, beautiful, and functional house. I was able to design a passive system that will allow air to flow throughout the birdhouse while enhancing its appearance.

Bird/Client: Black Capped Chickadee
Pritzker Architect: Renzo Piano

LANDON SCHOENECK

The inspiration for the design of this birdhouse is derived from Renzo Piano's concept of working with layers that fit together in a seamless manner, creating a form out of segments. The circular layers both reflect and fit tightly to the tree trunk. A removable top also functions as a birdbath, and thick walls create an elongated entry to protect the Black-capped Chickadee from predators.

Bird/Client: American Kestrel
Pritzker Architect: Shigeru Ban

LUKE GERDES

The inspirations for my birdhouse were from Shigeru Ban's main design philosophies: the manipulation of geometric shapes incorporating simple but complex elements. These very important characteristics were blended with the needs of the American Kestrel to create the birdhouse you see now.

Bird/Client: House Wren
Pritzker Architect: Zaha Hadid

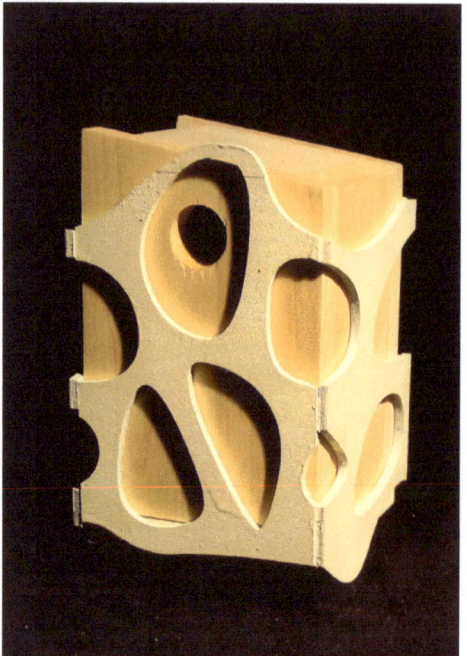

MATT THEISEN

This bird residence design was derived from the curved forms in the architect's style and the elegant patterns of spider webs – based on a symbiotic relationship between wrens and spiders. Through research, I found that wrens use spider eggs when constructing their nests so that the hatchling spiders will defend against parasites. The top of the house is removable so it can be easily cleaned each year.

Bird/Client: Tree Swallow
Pritzker Architect: Tadao Ando

MATTHEW PLASENTIA

I drew my inspiration from Tadao Ando's use of simple geometries and rectilinear forms, which reveal a much greater depth of thought as seen once inside his buildings. I created a beautiful simultaneous action and appearance of two boxes coming from one box, crafting hinges that moved in opposite directions, pulling one side out when the other was removed.

Bird/Client: White Breasted Nuthatch
Pritzker Architect: Rem Koolhaas

MITCHELL ABRAHAMSEN

My inspiration for the birdhouse came equally from the behaviors of the White-breasted Nuthatch, and from the design of the Bordeaux House by architect Rem Koolhaas. The nuthatch has a close relationship with the tree bark, searching for and storing nuts and insects. Just as beauty is revealed through simplicity, practicality and usefulness for the clients of Koolhaas, I made sure that the needs of the bird were also met.

Bird/Client: Eastern Screech Owl
Pritzker Architect: Thom Mayne

MITCHEL NYSTROM

I got inspiration for my birdhouse from architect Thom Mayne and his style of taking simple forms and morphing them to create complex forms. My inspiration from the Eastern Screech Owl came from its habit of using any opening it can find, and also from the bird's color and pattern on its feathers.

Bird/Client: House Wren
Pritzker Architect: I.M. Pei

MORGAN LARSON

A Wren's nest is bulbous and very spherical, which my inspiration came from, as well as the way the twigs spiral around the opening of the nest itself. Also inspired by I.M Pei's design process, I translated these aspects of the nest into geometric forms.

Bird/Client: White Breasted Nuthatch
Pritzker Architect: Richard Rogers

NICHOLAS SADDLER

I was inspired by architect Richard Rogers' ability to turn the structure of a building into something beautiful, functional, and unique. The A-frame structure of my birdhouse acts as a stand for the birdhouse while also holding up the roof. The hole is nestled between the pieces of the frame, based on the White-breasted Nuthatch's tendency to wedge nuts between bark to break them.

Bird/Client: Eastern Screech Owl
Pritzker Architect: Tadao Ando

RYAN TERSTEEG

I designed this birdhouse for the Eastern Screech Owl using the philosophies of architect Tadao Ando, who works with primarily concrete and wood, interlocking different shapes and spaces. Similar to Ando's buildings, my birdhouse relies on simple geometric shapes and just a little natural light since the owls are nocturnal. This window also allows the owl to look for prey from not only the front, but the side as well.

Bird/Client: Eastern Bluebird
Pritzker Architect: Oscar Niemeyer

SAMANTHA MARIHART

This birdhouse was inspired from the furniture inside the Palácio da Alvorada in Brazil, all designed by Oscar Niemeyer. Since this birdhouse was designed for the Midwest's Eastern Bluebird, a Native American influence was also incorporated. May the future of this house bring great joy to all birds that enter and provide them with the coolest little house on the block.

Bird/Client: House Wren
Pritzker Architect: Shigeru Ban

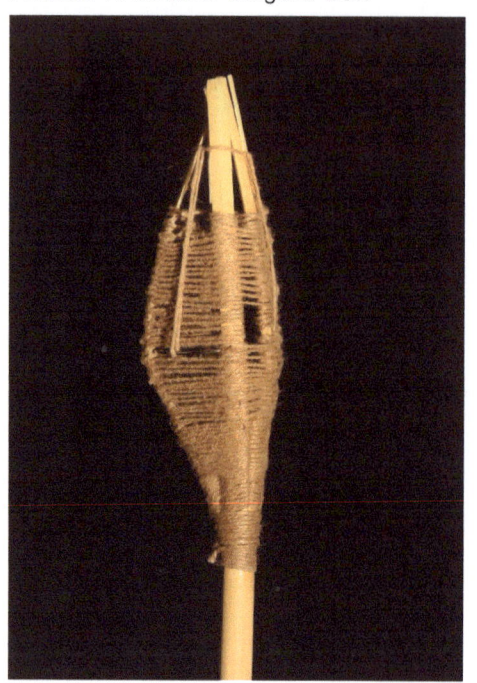

SARAH BIESTERVELD

The main inspiration for my design was Shigeru Ban's Furniture House 1, which integrated structure and furniture. I took this concept to the extreme and made the structure of my birdhouse double as the birdhouse itself. Ban chose his materials based on the region, so I used materials that were convenient to the bird, making my birdhouse as natural as possible.

Bird/Client: Tree Swallow
Pritzker Architect: Jean Nouvel

SHELLEY VANG

My inspiration was taken from Jean Nouvel's design of the Red Pavilion, where he focused on the context, materials, movement, and lighting for the structure. If designing a birdhouse for the tree swallow, I felt like Jean would be drawn to the color and shape of the bird, which I interpreted into structural shapes.

Bird/Client: House Wren
Pritzker Architect: Jean Nouvel

STINA OSTLIE

I was inspired by Jean Nouvel's modern style and his ability to create designs unique to their locations. Designing this birdhouse, it was important to keep the look and feel modern but also something habitable for a bird. I kept all the lines straight and simple and made the "bricks" of the birdhouse alternating tones to emphasize the horizontal layers of the wood. The birdhouse entrance is removable for cleaning and the top of the birdhouse is left open for ventilation.

Bird/Client: Black Capped Chickadee
Pritzker Architect: Rem Koolhaas

TANNER NAASTAD

The personality and needs of the Black-capped Chickadee, the style and design process of Rem Koolhaas, and the plains of North Dakota were my inspiration.

Bird/Client: Black Capped Chickadee
Pritzker Architect: Jorn Utzon

TY ENGLUND

When designing my birdhouse, I played with ways to connect the characteristics of the bird with my assigned Architect, Jorn Utzon. The walls of my birdhouse extend, instead of coming to a point, suggesting that the walls can be added to. The angular walls keep the eyes moving, playing off of the aerobic nature of the chickadee. Utzon also had believed that buildings should be more than just a standard box, so I took a box, and made a wall that appeared to be cutting through it.

Bird/Client: Eastern Bluebird
Pritzker Architect: Oscar Niemeyer

TYLER VOIGT

One of the things that drew Oscar Niemeyer's work together is the inspiration that arose from the natural scenery of Brazil. In creating a birdhouse for the Eastern Bluebird, I first took a look at the bluebird itself and the particular dimensions of houses Bluebirds like. Like Niemeyer, I used influences of simple underlying geometry, overlaid with complex curves.

Bird/Client: Tree Swallow
Pritzker Architect: Glenn Murcutt

ULYSSES SIBO

The inspiration for this birdhouse can be traced to two primary factors: the acrobatic maneuvering skills and beauty of the Tree Swallow, and the simplistic linear design that is often the characteristic of architect Glenn Murcutt's designs. True to his motto to touch the earth lightly, the birdhouse is constructed with materials that are favored by Murcutt.

Bird/Client: Tree Swallow
Pritzker Architect: Rafael Moneo

YINING FANG

The design philosophy is developed from Rafael Moneo, who regards the materials and techniques of construction to be just as important as the architect's vision and concept, and therefore an integral part of making architecture lasting. Building the Swallow Bowl is to offer the tree swallow a safe environment to breed when they are spending their time in the north part of America in the summer.

Bird/Client: White Breasted Nuthatch
Pritzker Architect: Norman Foster

ZACH MOEN

I was inspired by Norman Foster's RE Swiss Headquarters in London, which accommodates employee comfort with a design that takes advantage of daylighting and natural ventilation. I interpreted those philosophies into the design of a birdhouse to design a form that would sheer off harsh conditions, and allow birds the benefit of the positive weather.

BIRDS/CLIENTS

Black Capped Chickadee
White Breasted Nuthatch
Eastern Bluebird
Tree Swallow
House Wren
American Kestrel
Northern Flicker
Eastern Screech Owl

STUDENT CONTRIBUTORS

Javan Arroyo	John Krolak	Ty Englund
Sarah Biesterveld	Stina Ostlie	Benjamin Johnson
Jonathan Hegseth	Jacob Peterson	Samantha Marihart
Matthew Plasencia	Landon Schoeneck	Zachariah Moen
Elizabeth Rae	Huaxin Wei	Ulysses Sibo
Benjamin Zerrien	Kelsey Jarrett	Elizabeth Thordson
Jessica Meyer	Tyler Voigt	Drew Wolf
Tanner Naastad	Mitchell Abrahamsen	Ingrid Fullerton
Aaron Codden	Benjamin Gillis	Christa Galbraith
Jenna Hegedus	Hannah Langr	Luke Gerdes
Alexandra Mills	Alex Malnaa	Morgan Larson
Mitchel Nystrom	Julie Rasanen	Brady Laurin
Christopher White	Nicholas Saddler	Shelley Vang
Kaitlyn Aberle	Daniel Todd	David Walbolt
Hamza Elazhari Daoudi	Kenneth Stephenson	Jacob Hasse
Matthew Theisen	Yining Fang	Ryan TerSteeg

PRITZKER LAUREATES

Phillip Johnson	Alvaro Siza	Thom Mayne
Louis Barragan	Fumihiko Maki	Paulo Mendes de Rocha
James Stirling	Christan de Portzamparc	Richard Rogers
Kevin Roche	Tadao Ando	Jean Nouvel
I.M. Pei	Rafael Moneo	Peter Zunthor
Richard Meier	Sverre Fehn	Kazuyo Sajima & Ryue Nishizawa
Hans Hollein	Renzo Piano	Eduardo Souto de Moura
Gottfried Bohm	Norman Foster	Wang Shu
Kenzo Tange	Rem Koolhaas	Toyo Ito
Oscar Neimeyer	Jaques Herzog & Pierre de Meuron	Shingeru Ban
Gordon Bunshaft	Glenn Murcutt	Frei Otto
Frank Gehry	Jorn Utzon	
Aldo Rosi	Zaha Hadid	
Robert Venturi		

COMPETITION WINNERS 2015

Best Interpretation of Pritzker Architect's Philosophy:
1st place: Sarah Biesterveld (facing page, top)
Honorable mentions: Jake Hasse, John Hegseth

Best Suited to Bird Species:
1st place: Javan Arroyo (facing page, middle)
Honorable mentions: Jake Hasse, Ben Gillis

People's Choice Award:
Jake Hasse (facing page, bottom)

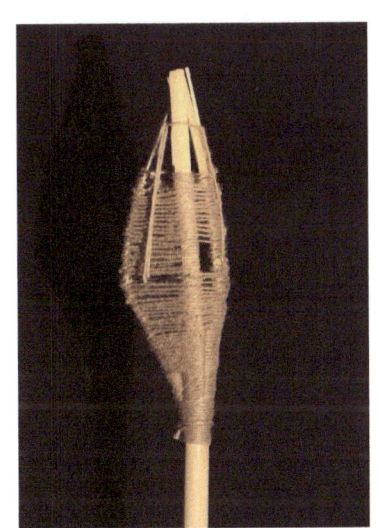

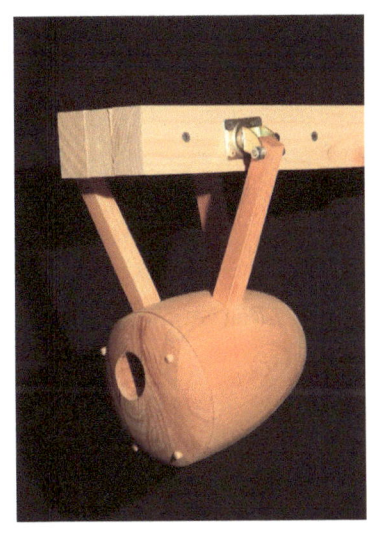

COMPETITION JURY

Chris Hawley, Architect
Ron Nellermoe, Ornithologist
Don Faulkner, Professor of Architecture

FACULTY ADVISORS

Joan Vorderbruggen, Assistant Professor, NDSU
Darryl Booker, Associate Professor, NDSU
Cindy Urness, Associate Professor, NDSU

NOTES

NOTES

NOTES

NOTES

NOTES

NOTES

www.ingramcontent.com/pod-product-compliance
Lightning Source LLC
Chambersburg PA
CBHW041814040426
42450CB00004B/154